ANCESTOR WORSHIP

ANCESTOR WORSHIP
Michael S. Begnal

salmonpoetry

Published in 2007 by
Salmon Poetry,
Cliffs of Moher, County Clare, Ireland
Website: www.salmonpoetry.com
email: info@salmonpoetry.com

Copyright © Michael S. Begnal, 2007

ISBN 1 903392 54 3

All rights reserved. No part of this publication may be reproduced or transmitted in any form or by any means, electronic or mechanical, including photography, recording, or any information storage or retrieval system, without permission in writing from the publisher. The book is sold subject to the condition that it shall not, by way of trade or otherwise, be lent, resold or otherwise circulated without the publisher's prior consent in any form of binding or cover other than that in which it is published and without a similar condition, including this condition, being imposed on the subsequent purchaser.

The cover shows a page from *Annála Ríoghachta Éireann (The Annals of the Four Masters)*, listing the death of Conaing Ua Beigléighinn, abbot of Kells, in the year 1128. The manuscript itself is dated to 1632. Reproduced with the kind permission of Acadamh Ríoga na hÉireann (The Royal Irish Academy).

Cover design & typesetting: Siobhán Hutson

Do m'athair,
i measc laochra na nGael go raibh sé

Acknowledgements

Some of the poems in this volume have appeared in the following magazines:

Apostasy Mag, *The Black Mountain Review*, *The Blue Canary*, *Books Ireland*, *The Brobdingnagian Times*, *The Burning Bush*, *College Green*, *Comhar*, *The Cúirt Journal*, *Cutting Teeth*, *Fortnight*, *The Galway Advertiser (Markings)*, *Icarus*, *Natural Bridge*, *Nerve*, *Orbis*, *Poetry Cornwall*, *Poetry Ireland Review*, *Poetry Scotland*, *Poetry Wales*, *Shearsman*, *The Stinging Fly*, *Translation Ireland*, *Vallum*, *west47*, *Wildeside*; and online in *Babel Magazine*, *Electric Acorn*, and *nthposition*.

Some of the poems in this volume have appeared in the following anthologies:

Breaking the Skin: 21st Century Irish Writing (The Black Mountain Press), *Go Nuige Seo* (Coiscéim), *Jacob's Ladder: An Anthology Underground* (Six Gallery Press), and *The New Galway Poets Anthology 1: Aphrodisiac Jacket* (privately printed).

The line, "A planet ain't a planet if it don't have wars" (p. 41), is a quotation from the song "Swan Lake" by Blackalicious.

Contents

Expatriation	9
Walled City	10
Three Visions of Pádraigín	12
Burned Hut	14
Irish Cities	15
Here in the West	16
S.F. Retrospect	17
View from a Galway Window	18
Cinco de Mayo	19
Madrileños	20
Montparnasse Cemetery	32
An Truailliú Nua	34
An Bhean Dheireanach	35
Ancestor Worship	36
My Role in Society	38
There's No Present	39
From Great Height	40
To the Gaelic People	44
Beautiful People	46
Prague Poems	48
Fuacht an tSamhraidh	52
Mothaím go bhFuil Mé chun Bás a Fháil	53
All Hours	54
Watching French TV5	55
Water Cress	56
Seal Poem	57
Old Men's Bar	58

Grianstad	60
Seal Poem	61
Ómós do na Peshmerga	62
Blues na Gaillimhe	63
Black, White, and Green	64
New Year's Day 1999	65
The Conquest of Gaul	67
Another Exile	70

Expatriation

Blue sky envelopes Galway
like the sea does Pádraigín
who drowned

American tourists sit
on the Claddagh bench
talking in Boston accents,
while a moth struggles uselessly
in the water
against its common death,
a kicking speck

like the oblivion of Boston,
cast from your gorted land
where rivers run free,
but not the minds
that aped their masters,
that aped their masters

and I too'm "American" now,
sauntering the local lanes,
land of ghostly progenitors,
cold stone,
bitter defeat

Walled City

Did I have the dream again
about the old walled city?
the blackened cobblestones
and wooden posts,
the winding passages
impregnable isolation

maybe my own childhood Prague,
where red and beige trams
sped down their lines,
distant dingy Gothic spires
out the fogged windows,
Russian tanks,
archways of stone,
public cages
where mediaeval criminals
were locked on show

or Cluj, where Balaban
kept a sheep head on the balcony,
waxen eyes glistening in the sun,
I hid in the gypsy cave
and threw sand at my brother,
I struggled pointlessly
in my eleventh-year limitations,
was taken screaming
along brown brick walls
to the Romanian barber
—or was he Magyar?

In the dream it's cold,
more like Galway,
its walls built by Normans

to keep out the Irish,
the aboriginal clans,
the fury of the Uí Flaithearta,
top dog tribe number one,
gates to admit no unwanted Ó or Mac

gates and towers,
now preserved in shopping mall,
or not preserved at all
and crumbling
stand bleakly by the Corrib,
remind for whom the city itself was founded
—I'm an Ó

though that's not in the dream,
just the city old,
black slated houses
up each twisting lane,
and the looming fortifications
that keep some in,
and some out

Three Visions of Pádraigín

1.

Pádraigín danced like a shaman
(on one leg),
his right eye bashed by cataract,
in the thrumming pipes
and drum summer night
of Cross St. stones

I was flipping a punt,
heads or harps,
which I gave him
when he came around collecting,
twinkle in his good eye,
shadow on his brow,
he looked like a man
plucked from early times,
a certain separateness
in his gait,
but when the music shrieked
he was back in his left mind

2.

He stood on the corner of Quay St.
baiting the police natively,
his white eye scrunched now,
the left straining out

> the cop of stone
>   silent in his duty,
> as unshakeable
>   as a Buckingham guard

As I walked up
he panhandled me quick
with his schizophrenic patois,
just some loose change
("Just to spite them")
and I had 15p,
three bulls—

"Níl focal ar bith acu
[they've not a word of Irish],"
he jabbed off his tongue,
his anger wrapped round
like a boxer's belted robe

3.

Same corner,
       the streets empty,
              air chilled silent

He leaned
against Neachtain's blue walls
in a grey wool overcoat,
we talked,
he always jumped languages,
always pent,
always spitting

Some circumstantial comrade
with a bottle of Buckfast,
or maybe Old Cellar,
approached and was brushed away
("Now leave us alone,
I'm talking Gaeilge to this one")
      (actual words)

but the Galway docks were waiting

Burned Hut

(An Spidéal, Cois Fharraige)
(waiting for the Galway bus)

Glass of the window
swims as you look
toward the Both Loiscthe bridge,
the language commandos
strike away English
on the Conamara road signs—
all the rivers
will bear their true names
in the dark of evening

all the villagers
will know
of what they speak
under the red rain
of their endless servitude,

and the waves lap
at the rock

Irish Cities

I sat in the Derry hotel room
above the city walls
on the eve of Imbolc
overlooking the Bogside hill,
slope of row homes,
big church,
traffic lights,
one massive ward
of the electoral city,
real working mass

like Waterbury, Connecticut,
where not I'm from
but my father
and all his fathers
since famine time in Fódla
—there they arrived
on a new phase of movement
like wave-battered Brendans
and populated,
planted the system within

disseminated,
the Go Nation

Here in the West

The dark stark "other" Galway,
desolate vapour fogs the head,
the smell of moist evening
while a white cat
lurks along the river
    at low tide

young men vomit their way
through the streets,
they swallowed
too much freedom
in malevolent mouthfuls
and traipse now
             time-blackened stone

a costumed couple
proceeds in a seedy direction
I follow (and see)

they're not costumed at all

S.F. Retrospect

A detail poet
performing, reporting the retrospect,
the story of how I got Here
(but not in that order):

still having those dreams
of back-on-Haight-for-the-first-time,
where they've changed the bars
and put in coffeehouses,
and rough-and-tumble raiders
work you in the project night

one of those,
where different blocks
mean other areas of awe

'cause just up the street
was my Mexican place,
Burrito Salvadoreño,
and a hot married Salvadoreña

I always got hot peppers,
always got hot peppers,
left impressive tips,
but feared the imagery
of the black Latin moustache,
murderous,
       vengeful husband

and deep in the Mission
it was even more dangerous
'cause you were
out of your language,
in deep down world

View from a Galway Window

Old World butcher shop
blue house
the rooftops
and smokestacks of crooked industry,
grey steeple
through the billowing steam
that blends into ugly
skies of repression
and clouds my window
like lace curtains

wires on rusted poles
tower above rickety man
(on his bike loaded down
with plastic bags full of lint)

the faint smell of sewage,
some girl ditches her dog
and a fat woman
heads for the beauty parlour,
open for Saturday business
this Bealtaine,
but all I see are
Mormon missionaries
sent severely from Utah

Cinco de Mayo

The closest I can get
right now to Mexico
is Texicanos corn chips,
"manufactured" (not baked)
in Coolock

but in Mexico
they crowd the streets
in painted faces howling
kicking dust and confetti,
eclipse us,
'course what do I know?
California
knows how to par-ade
and Aztlán
is slightly resettled

Madrileños

1.

Real Jardín Botánico—
bare feet getting some sun,
tufted clouds floating and I sneezed

cats, brown tiger strips, I mean stripes,
black and white friendly girl
smiles when you scratch the top of her ass,
hair all combed back and a little beard

L. bares dangerous flesh under a *Quercus macrocarpa*,
and lies on the altar-like stone bench

the Gran Vía has strip clubs

> had to kill that ant with a toe,
> out of his writhing misery (ant blood on my toe)
> (sun on my arm)

the kitty way down the path a-running along,
down beyond the sign for Aseos/Toilets

back of an ancient statue (I say ancient but I mean old),
my shoes to the left of me, flesh to my right,
leafy green *Phormium* behind (my arm is burning)

lines of Madrid,
       Second World,
             Graffiti

(pause to stare at the cat painted like a cow by nature)

I just seen Goya,
and Botticelli (women hunted through the trees),
and Jesus, and Mary squirting milk out of pornographic paps
(I only call it pornographic 'cause you get aroused)

live birds chirp now and whistle, food for cats (?),
shadow of the bush approaches my feet and
soon it will somehow swallow

2.

Because I, in my American, think of Mexico
I think Juárez while wandering:
metal balconies on buildings above,
adobe brown, shuttered for siestas,
bright flowers peek through iron railings,
red roof tiles

thin uphill streets lined with cervecerías,
eat tortilla yum egg patata onion,
wandering, restaurants full of pigs,
plates of fried squid in windows,
yellow mailboxes, fountains,
the policía on Calle de las Huertas,
submachine gun at Spanish hand,
my Spanish sunglasses, old ladies with canes

colour picture tile street signs remind of New Orleans,
but lottery vendor with tickets around his neck!

Tio Pepe, in big neon sign
that I remember while drinking sangria
(now I'm relaxed European, southern),
big Madrid shopping district,
homeless beggars one-armed on Calle Mayor

evening warmth,
red punch-coloured sangria wine
and lemon orange pieces floating in the pot

    nada nada nada

Goya's Saturn still in my head,
black, black, the picturas negras,
and I don't even know his history

but hey Ferlinghetti,
we seem to see,
in Goya we seem to see!

3.

Spray paint marker colour
graffiti on walls the green bus goes by,
    you drive on the right

to the station (Torrejón de Ardoz),
red in an industrial landscape,
Spanish pop radio on platform loudspeaker,
"yea a yeah yeah,"
concrete cement sidewalks and blocks
and round streetlights,
faraway scrub hills,
cranes for cold hollow construction

¡Attencion! a voice crackles,
interrupting the music,
though I no comprend but a couple words
and I don't mind, on the platform,
we's waiting for a train

back into the city past distant fields
with flowers of yellow and electrical metal pylons,
building sites and southern trees,
girders, shells of the places
where people abode themselves, toilers everyday

under the overpass, "California" again,
it's the language, highway,
and the air that hangs baking

ticket checker conductor comes for his prize
with metal punch holes,
    Gracias, gracias...

man in a maroon sweater reading *El Mundo*,
commuting into Madrid, outskirts, junk,
crabby patchy grass, rickety tile roofs in the old style,
Spanish architecture survives—
there was a war here among these dusty old buildings
    collapsing

(staying with friends outside the city we once again pull into)

4.

Bus to Toledo—
out onto a jaunting Madrid street
then the highway signs, apartment complexes and a
giant shiny ferris wheel,
yeah now we're hittin' the highway,
a wide six-laner, chugging down the Autovía,
it's like I live here

red poppies by the roadside,
the plains like Montana mud brick Arizona
(lets me pretend to be in America)

don't want to go home, I say, and debate with myself,
take a swig of agua bottle,
I don't really speak Spanish
just know a few words
but I can fake it pretty good

sleepy town along the route,
    quiet, pizza,
        stop for passengers,
            Spanish girls wear tight pants,
            Tele-Pizza

stop blank on the Calle de Generalisimo Franco
of another town,
be-flattened like the land,
the parched dirt moaning for rain,
shadows from the clouds/
I see myself sitting in the Bar Puerto Chico
alone, lost to the rest of the West,
or in any little Spanish bar with cerveza and a cold
egg

driver takes a leisurely pace and so we drift,
    make sketches in the mind,
        scenes, Miles, lazy trumpets,
    the girl sleeping in her seat,
thick raindrops in the sun,
    the new and the old,
        heavy army helicopters,
        heavy hand in the provinces

Toledo is revealed ahead,
a mountain behind,
snatches of red houses on a hill,
red earth, city on red earth
    "Groves"

5.

You don't know what you're getting yourself in for,
suddenly it's 1586, winding labyrinthine streets,
little cobblestones (but it's hot and sunny!)
(some wind), everything's at an angle

"Let's go to El Greco's house" (down the stepped stone lane)
(like one time El Greco lived there and his friends used to think:
"Yeah, I'm going to drop in and see El Greco"
in the city built on the hill)

came down to the little park,
smoked some hash in the stone monument,
you just stare across the canyon to the old rich houses on the hills,
look down at the river, ruins of an ancient bridge,
white
     wild
              geese tiny down on the far bank,

    City in Nature

and if you lived there
and this was your normal view
and the fog comes
and the snow—
you'd become completely separated from the world,
time mediaeval Spanish

Monasterio de San Juan de los Reyes,
an orange tree in the courtyard Gothic stone,
but the Church of Santo Tomé much smaller,
but a giant El Greco masterpiece in the dim light,
a middle-aged Spanish lady looks from a bench and weeps,
round the outside, out the thin paths of Moors,
separate, lost

    an orange cat alone,
    eye gouged in fight,
    waiting for help in the dry clay

6.

Sitting in the flat,
Torrejón high-rise, nine flights up,
Mahou beers still clinking in my head,
we sat in the bar smoking the brass pipe,
no one seems to mind or notice

wandered the financial district,
wandered again, the capital at night
not knowing whose sexual undertones,
we all sat on the puffy couch back room of La Comedia
remembering the scrapping drunks from before,
big muscle dude tryin' to restrain little loco guy,
girls at their sides,
      what's being said under flashing lights?

now I look down from the balcony,
people's clothes hung on the line across the way,
like the barking of a distant dog
can't even see Madrid now,
this a poor suburb, red brick developments,
yellow glass balcony partitions,
you can look out over all,
bird sounds from all ways

nothing to say, but I'm listening

I look across to the doorway
where a dark girl was dancing,
now is shut

(green bus calls me out)

7.

Sun on the tracks,
Bar El Extremeño, one of the rat traps
set among the pollerías, this-erías, that-etc.

the news vendor got mad at me—
I was reading the *USA Today* for free (no *Irish Times*),
he came up, hand held out,
I looked in his determined, bitter face,
put his paper back on the rack

Sol is the hub
downtown revolves around
(that one sentence or two?),
no, but Sol is sorta Times Square,
the big neon and lots of traffic

you see slogans that solidate with Peruvian rebels,
Che Guevara t-shirts in every rock stand,
plus Cuba and the EZLN, Chiapas postcards on a table,
no price, just a donation,
there was hot sun then, again, when I searched for shades

SE VENDE PISO signs on balconies,
we could get a flat, move in,
be a subject of the king,
cook some tortilla in a frying pan,
even take siestas, chillin' out in old Iberia
with old men across the hall and noisy pipes,
········wood shutters,
················a nosebleed

Old Spain by the railroad tracks
(I harp on, out in the scummy suburbs)
(the ghetto outside)

so old, Spain, I see, ain't like anywhere—
they keep strange hours
and stay crazy

8.

Colour tile metro stations,
Madrid's a city of monuments,
Plaza de España, a giant Quixote,
Sancho Panza trailing in live bronze
and stately Cervantes looks on above

then an old lady in a red-striped dress and sunglasses
climbs under the horses
and her husband takes her photo
(finally posed at Quixote's sharp spur),
her slip shows when she crawls out and she laughs in French
(I see them drinking coffee in the Paris 1960s)

L. sports a European white-scarf-on-head,
not Ireland at all, not a cloud,
      clear little pond

traipsed back to Sol,
"Está Usted en la Zapatería Mas Barata de Todo España"
says the sign in the cheapest shoe store in all Spain

Taberna Celta in the alley, corner of
Calle de Santa María y Costanilla de los Desamparados,
plaques of all Celtic countries, Guinness sign outside,
but closed at 5:30 in the afternoon!
so farther down to a little plaza
where sparrows flit on the sandy ground,
small footprints, sounds of a gurgling fountain,
griffons continually spewing aqua eruption,

two sparrows sit tail to tail (they're friends),
pigeons look for crumbs as shadows of tree leaves
pass back and forth like speckled curtains,
some kid yelping

(I might have had a reincarnation,
a son of Míl making ready to sail,
the land is so flat open—
we were pushed out)

9.

Big park to smoke in,
but Spanish police in navy blue with guns at the hip
look mean—gotta dodge, quick do it
and cut to the big stone steps,
there's a film crew on location,
drums across the lake, a quartet playing hacky-sack,
every person hanging out
(they really know how to hang out),
it's one of the great cities
(baby spiders on my arm)

a guy carrying his bag on a stick
over his shoulder like a vagabond
watching the hacky-sackers—
but he's a well-dressed silver gentleman,
interested, ready to try his hand

the film crew tapes off one side,
some homeless guy (young)
stumbles around shouting his language

moustachioed fellow in dark glasses
(you could sit here and / watch forever)

a coupla tourists, lolling rowers oar in,
oar pops up wet and dripping,
bright white reflections shoot across the water,
gypsies drinking a big brown bottle,
hippies, "intense" people,
Africans there at the drums, big circle,

suddenly bagpipes fade in!

10.

Red sun in evening, bricks still hot,
      long angular shadows,
            red

slot machine games in every little cheap bar

milk truck: Celta/Leche de Galicia,

we were *madrileños*

thinking about the girls, sex, edgy,
going back in a taxi, thinking backward,
light down on thigh she felt

copper curvy pipe,
instruments utilized in restaurant toilets,
dour Chinese waiter,
we late customers making funny faces,
cold wind for Spain / really is the place
(tell us about the girls)
      (can't, I'll be in trouble)
(c'mon!)
      (*irlandés*, ogled in the park,
even crazies sometimes show taste)

(man, I wouldn't mind going on a little)

vegetarian place,
yeah that's when J. first made his face:
"The waitress has been watching us
so I'm giving her a serious look"
and A. funnily incredulous

black curly hair of the tightly t-shirted waitress
and we eat our fake meat

we used the instruments that time too,
and then later again in the open in a bar,
it was the funny rock bar that we brought beers out of
to drink at the flat, last night,
and boy was I bushed, heck
and I knew not much was gonna happen,
but didn't care

Spanish McDonalds,
we waiting for them,
Sol, patatas fritas on the menu

(I've discovered my spontaneity)
(alright, m'man's discovered his spontaneity!)

faceless fighter pilots blow their jets over Torrejón,
over bullrings, the swimming pool,
growling Alsatian in the local bar,
       and now we's out

Montparnasse Cemetery

You get overwhelmed
by a city ideal beauty,
hardly a minute to think about death,
though everybody does—
the old man at Montparnasse Cemetery
in the empty tombhouse,
safe from the rain
but not for long

think of all the bridges on the Seine,
that melancholy snake,
men and women have jumped off,
insignificants splash
in the green murk,
tempted

in the hotel room bed
I sit out the rumbling showers
watching French TV under pink blankets
remembering my wet birthday,
sex show fatigue at Pigalle,
trudging in leaky shoes a city old,
and I've grown a moustache—
I do seem respectable, I think,
drinking Dr Pepper in

pink marble columns Paris,
like, for example, l'Arc du Carrousel
and Place St-Michel,
all monuments to dead soldiers

but let's all forget about that
and admire the art, no?
the glory of France's war dead
dazzles me, frankly,
so I stand awed
at the city made beautiful
by these many nameless extinctions

I eat bread
that reminds me of: "Cock"
and drink water
that hangs heavy on my hands
and wear out my soles
just to make it to a place
where writers are laid
and to think,
"Just a few feet down,
his actual bones"

Baudelaire's grave
covered with green Métro tickets,
many-coloured flowers,
and a sketch—
Beckett's bare—
Sartre's respectable—

> cemetery toilets smell
> like fermenting forest piss,
> and flies congregate in gangs,
> waiting to eat your shit

An Truailliú Nua

Beifear ag caint faoin "seanairgead"
creid é nó ná creid—
braithfidh muid uainn
   na héin,
      a gcleití
         ina slaodanna,
na bradáin ag snámh
ar scatháin beaga,
bod mór an tairbh,
an t-each foighneach
ag fanacht lena mharcach

agus níorbh fhiú é
a bheith i do scríbhneoir
agus Joyce bainte den *tenner*
(foirgneamh leamh ina ionad)

agus cé go bhfuil mo shloinne
luaite in *Annála Ríoghachta Éireann*,
is éigean dom glacadh
leis an truailliú nua

An Bhean Dheireanach

Gruanna bána mar phoirceallán,
a cuid gruaige rua as réamhstair,
súile doimhne fiáine,
aghaidh Hipearbóranach,
an bhean dheireanach

tá cuma ársa uirthi—
b'iad na haoiseanna
a rinne a cuid féitheog is féith is matán,
craiceann bog bán sínte
ar chnámha bána sinseartha

siúlann sí de chois
trí chathair choincréite,
iarsma den am
nuair a bhí cónaí
ar a muintir
i measc na gcarraigeacha

Ancestor Worship

Not like the bones of parents
carried out in procession
from their dark vaginal tombs
among the rocks,
mummified skin stretched
and tanned in mockery of death

it's not like the imagined
rituals of an old old age
before iron or bronze,
the metal of our mythology,
though the faces look the same
in the rain

but the warm blood
that flows through to this age,
dangerous and violent in veins,
hanging heavy like burlap sheets
on a dewy day

the right hook of history,
the slow motion arc of the punch,
the strange figure
on a modern city street
who burrows into your eye
and says, "Who're you?"

It's like when Lennon laid
his *New York* album on you,
and appeared in pictures
in his new image—
Revolutionary,
sudden Irishman,
Manhattanite,

gritty...

like LeRoi Jones's move to Harlem,
broke with his white friends,
changed his name:

> ancestor worship
> is the only religion
> truly compatible
> with the fact
> of evolution

My Role in Society

Ain't no carving of victuals to pop radio
    standing on bleachy tile floors,
ain't no furious pounding of metal into rock,
    helmeted, marooned on the rig,
ain't no soaking sinks of yellowy dishwater,
ain't no feverish work in the oil of night—

but I boogie down when I please,
in fact sometimes
       I sit in the grass,
       in the blades,
       bees,

and bug out
in the bug-out zone
with a beer, a hurley,
and go back thousands

cannibalize myself,
I wrote days ago some of these lines,
of life in the field
            (writ large)

orange butterfly,
       flutter soul

            sun scan

            scun

    my role in society,
    oh I know it
    oh why know it

There's No Present

There's no present
just a continual becoming
past

(hot sun on the Paddy's Day parade,
S.F. '94, bo-ing out, ass on the kerb,
collection for the cause,
free newspapers)

now,
oh now is gone,
then, in front of an electric fire
I'm slanging it all over the place,
cash rules everything 'round
while the twilight flows
in from the Border

and girls with red faces
   sit in the diffused light
      of steamy air that
         was

From Great Height

In the time of the flying ants
a twilight streetlamp moulders pink,
pink as the clouds upon grey air,
pink as one's vulva in magazines,
soft as the smell of lily
in the eternal Connacht summer,
she is a great explosion of hair,
she is someone's tender moment in a life full of shock,
it is a fine music the rumble of wings,
she (that cat) is taut sleek muscle
a natural aesthetic of fur under a car,
I am an aesthete, I am high,
and I've got three realms of thought plus
one controls the mix in turntable scratch,
and I tell you now that
in the time of the winged snakes
I was a black ibis at mountain pass,
seen now in the veins of streets
with winged ants ellipsing the head,
fondly standing, yes, bring on the bats

Looking over a city
and the gulls of Gaillimh at great height,
see a broad sweep, such a one as this,
a crane arm idle green
the caked green of the distant dome
the hill estates sprawled and maroon
the silent sea sailed upon,
on car-park Level Six, the roof,
you attempt to get ill, like
a brother in the Irish Basketball Association,
two a team, black,
show those white guys a thing or two
working the angle of the homeboy in the IBA
bears certain orthographic resemblance
to a certain army of freedom fighters,
"A planet ain't a planet if it don't have wars,"
said my man with the gift of gab,
this I know to be true
from great height, such as this
do not seek the Way Out

One controls the mix in turntable scratch,
resemblance seen now in the veins of others,
an explosion eternal, tender she is
sprawled and soft such as summer fur,
great as the smell upon grey air,
at mountain pass wars I tell you of association,
the man with a long arm, black of freedom,
stretching the angle of a city
still she is away like in the natural army,
music the rumble, Irish our own strength,
taut sleek muscle to be true,
we do not seek the roads in magazines,
streets not for the silent show
but a planet full of shock
in the time of distant fighters,
pink as the clouds before someone's been taken
ill under a car, and the gulls of hair,
a twilight moment in a life you attempt,
at great height you are softly whatever again
drinking from the stream of the dead

The giant mound's been taken again
whatever now its name, Cruach/Croagh,
but we climb up always the same
not for the monotheists, I prefer the *Samildánach*
and there were others still before,
it's for the pain in the calves
for to be high up in another place
with the high-flying crow, still higher
we be like airline passengers
looking down on fields, the roads,
our own strength's what put us here
and we will not be coptered away
like a broken-legged tourist,
in the stretching of the tendon
you are softly removed from the web,
lofted with a long arm,
drinking from the stream of technology,
the carrying of the stick,
the dead sheep rotting in the meadow,
O! so much preparation for the going down

To the Gaelic People
(translated from the Irish of Mícheál Óg Ó Longáin, 1800)

To the Gaelic people: MOVE!
Don't stop till daybreak—
extinguish, destroy, shatter, crush
towns and houses of the English-speaking race,
    the menial, wretched rabble
    who have sapped your purpose—
what an embarrassment it would be for you
(who are descendents of kings)
    if you submit to them.

    What biting anguish to see
    the Gaelic race in this sorry state,
a once happy people, exuberant,
now apathetic, listless and weak,
    without proper clothes or food
    or even a meal on the table,
while these boors sit snugly
and soundly in our homes—
    the very thought is torture.

    Listen just a little more
    and don't interrupt,
you ain't heard nothing yet.
That crowd of gangsters in your midst
    has spewed forth this misery,
    but get yourselves ready for them—
there's an army as powerful as a flood
coming to you across the sea
    that will put an end to your suffering.

Many thanks to the Son of the Virgin
for those of us remaining active,
now sworn together, unrelenting,
and prepared to make a radical move.
Do not ever cease
until every road is clear
and the boors are sent running
(streaming piss and shit)
back out of Ireland.

Ó Longáin's Note: In the year 1800 I recited this poem urging/inciting the Gaels to come with me and take vengeance on our oppressors. Unfortunately it was to no avail, as it didn't stir them in the slightest. This is not to say they wouldn't rise again if the French (or some similar help) were to arrive, as has often been promised us. But there was near-famine in Ireland at the time, with a measure of potatoes costing half a crown, and eight or nine shillings for a peck of meal, etc.

Beautiful People
(for Robert Reid)

Dead bird blown down the road
as light as its feathers,
the cops rousted a guy
and hung him over the river
on my way up to
where it was all happening

making me paranoid
with their gestapo patrols
so I try my power of observation
on the swans, majestic
in the sun,
and ready to kill any duckling
that gets in their way

then I saw you
on the theatre steps,
foaming at the mouth,
putting sweat from the pores
of your face
like a steelworker,
or a chaingang rockbreaker,
in fact you were on the lam

and when you walked toward town
with your maybe girl,
shrinking imperceptively with each step,
I noted that scene
more than any others,
despite the summer crowd
t-shirts and American shorts
movie star shades

erect nipples
and burning red shoulders,
I hung back among it all
and watched unknown,
being watched myself somewhere,

    maybe a second-storey window
    where sat someone
    slitting the skin of a pomegranate,
    the knife dripping with juice

Prague Poems

1.

Red orange and copper green
dot dot dot rooftops,
tile forest and trees
pierced by Vltva grey

brick castle battlements
under the nose
of rifled guards
in blue guardhouse costume,
the Castle,
hrad cobbles,

and the guards nearly
crack up laughing
when they look
at each other
changing

2.

Pointed spires by night
haunt one mediaevally,
the devil lurks around
corners and deep cellars

you see him on statues,
houses,
in the form of a red lamb
or grey ram,
   horns and
   pointed ears

Galerie Kamzík stickers
on glass windows
(Mona Lisa horned)

The Castle looms above
and lanes snake down
to the stony squares,
Nerudova's torn-up mosaic sidewalks

Too much Amerika,
too many shorts-wearers,
oblivious to their own
   incongruity

3.

When the rain comes
it soaks the rocks black
and leathers barbarian faces

stains seep in
wooden floors,
strollers stand in doorways
and watch wet passers,
some of whom act
as if there was no rain,
clothes drenched, yet
outwardly indifferent,
knowing the sun will soon
steam it all away

4.

Distant forests
where wild boars rummage
pine needles
and sharp sky Slavs

Pheasants fly,
feathers long,
      from
        tree
        to
        tree

Fuacht an tSamhraidh

Solas donn ag lonrú anuas
thar cosáin scoilte chathair na hoíche,
na foirgnimh liatha a phlúchann an radharc—
tarraingím mo chaipín olla thar mo shúile dá thoisc,
an dhuilleog chomh híseal nó go dtagaim,
in aice na habhann, chugam féin aríst /

labhróinn leat le srón-ogham,
ag comharthú le méara ar chaol mo shróine
agus comharthófá ar ais chugam,
ár stór focal ag gluaiseacht tríd an aer
       go ciúin,
               ciúin,
                      ciúin,

  "tá mé buailte ag an ghaoth…
mar sliotar ar bhos an chamáin…buailte
 …fuacht an tsamhraidh…fuacht…"

Mothaím go bhFuil Mé chun Bás a Fháil

Mothaím go bhfuil mé chun bás a fháil
an t-am ar fad

agus mé ag dul, dul, dul,
fós níl aon shlándáil nó sábháilteacht
le lorg san fhilíocht,
na focail nárbh fhéidir liom a scaoileadh
a ritheann anois mar abhainn bhán chasta
sa dorchadas

deilbh éiginnte ar an mbruach

Mothaím go bhfuilim ag fáil báis i gcónaí
ach dearbhaím nach staonfaidh mé,
cén fáth go staonfainn agus an corp beo fós:
na cíocha ag luascadh, an áilleacht sin,
agus an fhuil ag luchtú an bhoid,
craiceann ag fliuchadh, ag glioscarnach

ceol ag foluain san aer mar sholas tathagach

Mothaím go bhfuil mé chun bás a fháil
agus gheobhaidh mé bás go luath,
ní ach pearsa amháin mé
as na mílte glúin a síolraíodh is a d'éag,
dúradán ar an scáileán,
file ag cur focal ó m'inchinn ghlóthach gheal

agus an dán seo dorn i do bhéal

All Hours

An olive-green felt couch
beamed in dim light hum,
Irish Times tossed down
and the still-life flowers
drying

all hours in the night—
the scratched eyes,
the olive sky,
and, say
there was linoleum down

a peeking ashen grey
through the tree leaves,
ugly branches almost bare—
so summer ends,
endless gnarling,
die again and again

say it was home,
say it was college,
that was now
this was now
was now

what it is is
the silence,
no stimulati sticking your ears,
says my other mouth,
other man

Watching French TV5

Watching French TV5
I strain to penetrate the sound barrier
extracting random phrases but no coherent sentences,
only the gist of Jesus—
it's a panel of intellectuals debating religion,
a priest proud in his black suit,
and it's all capped off by the blonde soul singer
with her gospel smash "Walls of Jericho,"
Black America in her breast when she sings,
then the Gallic tremule of her speech
as she rejoins the fray

I wonder, says me,
to myself of course,
to L. if she were awake,
what's going on in Paris—
in the Québécois bookshop,
or the gable roof flat windows
showing naked occupants,
and all the expression

that I am denied

Water Cress

Ways that I'm not like a bard,
ways that I'm like a satirist
suffering the slings of myself,
my vast torpidity
and inevitable disgust
at the exclusion practiced
       by myself
       and others

hazy figures
passing my window,
local girls in blue skirts

O the sneers
on O'Brien's Bridge,
I see the silver bird
with the spotlight on my face
in the raw sopping night air,
and the drooping grey houses
of untold construction

and three lads who
I thought were butch lesbians,
freaky costumes
(where do they get their walks?),
a can of beer,
a guard at the theatre door,
suddenly I don't care
       like a cat

water cress, water cress
over on the hostile side of town

Seal Poem

I don't understand my dreams

Day spent watching seals in the river,
speckled heads bobbing through the surface,
curious faces peering over to the shore,
the built stone banks, the bridge,
and diving down again for fish,
dive-bombing seagulls plummeting
all around them

The cool thing is to make eye contact
with an inquisitive seal—
of course they have emotions,
curiosity is one—
and to give her a human name,
Speckle-head, or to get really serious
about it, *Breac-chinn*

At night I'm in a high-rise apartment building
with Jerry Seinfeld and some girls,
and someone pulled off his wig
revealing his blond crew-cut,
which just about ended everything

Old Men's Bar

Salmon-pink walls, this fishy room,
these stuffy cushioned booths
(I'm tolerated),
old men pouring the water jug,
whiskeying their innate suspicion of writers,
fellas in caps just shooting the shit,
"Can you read without the glasses?"

(I'm furtive—
if they caught me they'd raise a shaking fist)
cotton in the ears, soaking up the pus,
the excess wax of their progressing diseases

whiskey cure,
one beetle recognizes another,
"Ya from Galway?"
old man to another

pour the whiskey with shaking hand
into trembling lips, slow,
so the top of the glass fogs up
from nosed breath

television on like in Earwicker's,
the barman changes the channel
to an *Oprah* audience scene:
"Blacks," says a drinker

sexless trio in the middle
of cunt-coloured painted walls,
dead wives,
creeping stink of age,
glasses of beer,

        raincoats,
                galoshes,
                        neckties

"…they called him Smitty,
over in Manchester…"

all the action is at the bar,
and they come in
in afternoons of ash,
wet mists swirling
over bare head skulls,
a new arrival,
wisps of white hair yellowing,
tapping fingers,
skin stretched on bone

headlights are on
in the November twilight,
the rush of wet tires outside

barman switches it again,
to a news story,
an elephant who paints pictures

Grianstad

Asleep on the bank
the sun stopped,
shone on the tiger cat

black cat sat leopard-like
basking in orange
on a thick tree limb
turned crimson

sat meditating
on the shortest day
and the stream slowly flowed,
sat thinking on the hung sun

and some pine somewhere
still shouted out:
Green!

Seal Poem

His family all dead
a lone brown seal toils against
the Corrib—that bitch—rushing mad to sea,
fast, humans are nauseous looking at her

but the seal is heading upstream
like some kinda Sisyphus,

       plodding up out of a wave,

and plop, back in, the cold brown water
wants to kill our fellow mammal

taker of suicides the river

the seal snorts water back out the nostrils,
not even evolved a blowhole,
more like an aquatic canine, our friend,
the strength of his spine
as he kicks his flippers,
               splosh,

is it for fish he angles over to the side
by the tower?

Ómós do na Peshmerga

Fir na hairde glaise/
    mná na nglérosc
ag tabhairt aghaidh ar an ghaoth,
ag siúl trí fhéar na sléibhte,
ag athghabháil línte dofheicthe na léarscáile

nó in Kirkuk, AK-eanna ag bladhmadh san aer,
trucail i ndiaidh trucaile ag plódú isteach,
céim amháin chun tosaigh ar an chos ar bolg

cos i ndiaidh coise,
    an ghrian os a gcionn

Blues na Gaillimhe

I mo shuí sa seomra,
níl ag breathnú ar an teilifís,
ciúnas i mo thimpeall,
tonnta mara amuigh i gcéin

i rith na hoíche—
sciathán leathair ag eitilt
cois an droichid

Black, White, and Green

Last summer I floated in the Boyne
eyes wet on the crest of a wave,
that milk was sweet and white
but the voices that came from my mouth
were black as a blackbird's beak at Midnight

you fathomed my advance
when we stepped out on the sward,
your skin was so visible
under a gaze, raw in my hand,
you knew simultaneously how we got to where
now we are at—
because Australopithecus walked on two legs,
stripped off the leafy canopy

we drank each other and saw

this summer the night fell again,
the darkness played green shadows
on your face, your hair,
I looked not unlike all my forebears
when they are my age, and though sleeping,
you proclaimed the future of
your people liberated

New Year's Day 1999

In the search for Hell's Kitchen
the wide westside streets
lay hollow in the cold

to breathe,
    an assault:
each moment hard
as the metal face
of a 10th Ave. payphone

always the streets, of course,
always the streets,
as I sought a "street" culture,
the traces of its bitterness,
the green neon of its bars,
the canny underdog,
the White Negro,
the setting of antipodal rivalries,
compression

But the westside streets
lay hollow,
broken liquor bottle,
each year the same
solid pavement,
frozen streams of canine
    and primate
        piss

they all left because of money,
their slice of the hair pie,
full integration:
Lucky Charms for breakfast,
and shower with Irish Spring—

I only turned east
(at an alien corner)
because of the temperature,
the Janus-month extremity
of the situation,
noted
another empty bottle,
Baileys in a doorway,
a brown paper bag,
warehouse,

    the monstrous ramp

The Conquest of Gaul

> *I am working hard to bring over the tribes which are standing aloof from us. The whole of Gaul will then be united, and when we are all of one mind the entire world cannot stand against us.*
>
> Vercingetorix, 52 B.C.
> (quoted by Caesar, *De Bello Gallico*)

In the jet light of dusk tide
glowers the industrial office,
soviet in its shabby savage plan
this ziggurat at bus stops,
> across the scrub lot land,
> the prickers, wire tangling at feet,
> burned charcoal log, nettled,
> breeze block then
> over the frosty wall

Don't get hit

And I miss the lost mistletoe recipe
this time of year, the customs
retained yet forgotten,
hung up on doorways—
winter, like the women at Gergovia,
breasts bared to plead, Gaulish, pale,
hale in their ardour,
missing, missing all—
> secretly I know what it is
> to be under onslaught,
> the fire from another hill,
> be bottlerocketed or
> be it centurion,
> always comes camaraderie

Kid, you gonna get hit,
by modern-day managers who want
to break your will
to restrict you by contract
and you know that's not MAT,
       that's not MAT

So they assail you
in warehouse districts dark,
so you are slowly separated,
so civilizations fall and rise
in cyclic defeats,
customs forgotten yet retained,
       I don't know how I'll go on,
       I feel how, instinct-like,
       I'm writing lines as I drift—
       back over the wall, kid

The walk home in pitch
through the bushes moist,
their green shrubby leaves
untrimmed like pubic hair
of Gaulish women, wild,
dark passages always attract
the shaft of light,
there are ritual and
not so ritual fuckings

But always rain,
the deluge, no ceremonies at all
of mistletoe or mare
in the shadow of modern commerce,
the shadow under which I walk
broke   busted   beaten
as that girl on the bus, black-haired,
glimpses of her face not for me,
her mare-like face in its beauty

fades as I pass local youths,
territorial on their road
by the condos under construction,
hatching a life of crime—
so I put on my tough walk,
breeze right by
and hit town

Hit? Hit back,
lay your head on no cement pillow

Our fuckings are individual,
breasts still sway and shake and
bodies soak in camaraderie,
the soaked flesh intensely perishable
lust lush will outlast the brick
of the industrial estate,
and the nation of Gaul still live
when every empire has been turned
       to crumbs

Another Exile

At times I sense our forefathers' graves,
holes in the earth rotten with the meat of the dead,
decaying skin that hallows the land,
that nourishes grass blades on the hills,
the rolling green ridges,
the shooting stalks that rustle in the breeze,
binding me to a country

other times I'm given to movement,
the smooth days of exile that arrive in foreign regions,
the inevitable throes of distance,
some city perhaps:
the line broken / all forgotten?
              NO,
   but everything transformed,
       the line bending,
         curving,
   the burden being lightened